UNITED KINGDOM

BY CARLA MOONEY

Essential Library
An Imprint of Abdo Publishing
abdobooks.com

ABDOBOOKS.COM
Published by Abdo Publishing, a division of ABDO, PO Box 398166, Minneapolis, Minnesota 55439.

Printed in the United States of America, North Mankato, Minnesota.
102022
012023

Cover Photos: Shutterstock Images (Big Ben, pattern)
Interior Photos: Ingus Kruklitis/Shutterstock Images, 4–5; Daniel Lange/iStockphoto, 6; Hesther Ng/SOPA Images/Sipa USA/AP Images, 7; Dron G./Shutterstock Images, 8; iStockphoto, 10, 19, 23, 34, 55, 98; Jon Super/AP Images, 12; Shutterstock Images, 14–15, 26–27, 54, 59, 63, 77, 81, 88–89, 94, 101; Peter Hermes Furian/Shutterstock Images, 16 (United Kingdom); Web Tools/Shutterstock Images, 16 (globe); Daniel Eskridge/Shutterstock Images, 21; Sol Stock/iStockphoto, 25; Helen J. Davies/Shutterstock Images, 28; Daniel Rao/iStockphoto, 29; Stephen Bridger/Shutterstock Images, 31; Lukas Zdrazil/Shutterstock Images, 32; Peter Cripps/Alamy, 36–37; Radomir Rezny/Shutterstock Images, 39; Dave Head/Shutterstock Images, 40–41; Science & Society Picture Library/Getty Images, 44; AP Images, 49; Carrie Davenport/Getty Images Entertainment/Getty Images, 50–51; Hulton Deutsch/Corbis Historical/Getty Images, 53; Max Mumby/Indigo/Getty Images Entertainment/Getty Images, 56–57; Eddie Mulholland/AFP/Getty Images, 64–65; zz/KGC-178/Star Max/Ipx/AP Images, 67; House of Commons/PA Wire/AP Images, 70; Michael Tubi/Shutterstock Images, 71; Claire Doherty/Alamy Live News/Alamy, 73; Tejas Sandhu/MI News/NurPhoto/AP Images, 75; Matthew Horwood/Getty Images News/Getty Images, 76; Everett Collection/Shutterstock Images, 78–79; William Perugini/Shutterstock Images, 82; Africa Studio/Shutterstock Images, 83; Maciej Olszewski/Shutterstock Images, 85; Russell Moore/Alamy, 86; M. Unal Ozmen/Shutterstock Images, 90; Richard Walker/PA Wire/AP Images, 92; Mark Kerrison/In Pictures/Getty Images, 97

Editor: Alyssa Sorenson
Series Designer: Maggie Villaume

Library of Congress Control Number: 2022940377

PUBLISHER'S CATALOGING-IN-PUBLICATION DATA
Names: Mooney, Carla, author.
Title: United Kingdom / by Carla Mooney
Description: Minneapolis, Minnesota: Abdo Publishing, 2023 | Series: Essential Library of Countries | Includes online resources and index.
Identifiers: ISBN 9781532199509 (lib. bdg.) | ISBN 9781098274702 (ebook)
Subjects: LCSH: United Kingdom--Juvenile literature. | Europe--Juvenile literature. | Great Britain--History--Juvenile literature. | Geography--Juvenile literature.
Classification: DDC 941--dc23

CONTENTS

CHAPTER **ONE**

A TOUR OF THE UNITED KINGDOM

It's midmorning when the plane touches down at Heathrow Airport in London, England. Sarah rubs her eyes and stretches after the long transatlantic flight from New York. She slips her backpack straps over both shoulders and follows her parents and brothers into the bustling airport. Heathrow is the United Kingdom's largest airport and the busiest one in Europe. Sarah grins with excitement; her family's United Kingdom adventure has begun.

A taxi carries Sarah's family from the airport to the flat they have rented for the week. Standing on the flat's balcony, Sarah can see the River Thames, one of

London is a sprawling city with a long, rich history.

River boats take passengers down the River Thames.

Millions of people go on the London Underground each day.

the longest rivers in the United Kingdom. The Thames flows hundreds of miles through many of England's towns, passes through the city of London, and eventually empties into the North Sea. The riverbank is busy with pedestrians walking to their destinations, while boats and river buses travel up and down the river.

Sarah's stomach rumbles. She's ready for lunch. The family walks a few blocks from the flat to the nearest subway station. The London Underground, also known as the Tube, is an underground railway

The London Underground links approximately 270 subway stations throughout London.[1]

system that carries passengers throughout the city of London. The London Underground's first underground railway opened in 1863. It was 3.75 miles (6 km) long, connecting Farrington Street and Bishop's Road in Paddington. The line was a success from its opening and carried 9.5 million passengers in its first year alone. In the 1900s, the London Underground expanded and new lines were added. At the start of the 2000s, the lines of track reached approximately 250 miles (400 km), and more than one billion passengers rode the London Underground annually.[2]

Sarah and her family ride the next subway train to central London. They walk a few blocks on the London streets and stop at a pub for lunch. Sarah decides to order one of England's most well-known dishes: fish-and-chips. Fillets of cod are covered in a light batter and fried to create a crispy, juicy treat. The chips are thick-cut potatoes also fried and smothered in salt and vinegar. Next to them is a classic side dish of mushy peas, which are soaked overnight and simmered with sugar to create a thick, green mash. It's delicious, and Sarah eats everything on her plate.

ORIGINS OF FISH-AND-CHIPS

The tradition of eating fish-and-chips in the United Kingdom dates back to the early 1800s. It is believed that Jewish immigrants brought this way of cooking fish to the United Kingdom from Portugal and Spain. The fried fish became so popular it even appeared in Charles Dickens's classic 1838 novel *Oliver Twist*. The earliest record of chips in the United Kingdom is from 1860 in the English city of Oldham. In the 1860s, shops in London and Lancashire began to sell a meal of fish-and-chips. The dish was a hit, and by 1930 there were tens of thousands of fish-and-chips shops across the United Kingdom.

A CITY OF LANDMARKS

After lunch, Sarah's family climbs onto a red double-decker bus and sits on the upper deck. London is a city with hundreds of bus routes, and many buses travel past some of the city's landmark sights. The bus passes several places that Sarah has read about, including St. Paul's Cathedral, Trafalgar Square, the Houses of Parliament, and Westminster Abbey. She can't wait to spend more time at these sites in the coming days.

Sarah and her family disembark the bus at Victoria Station, one of London's central railway and Underground stations. At the station, Sarah's family rents a car and heads out for an afternoon trip in the English countryside. They drive to the English county of Wiltshire, about 90 miles (145 km) west of London.

HISTORY OF THE DOUBLE-DECKER BUS

The first double-decker bus appeared on the streets of Paris, France, as a two-level horse-drawn carriage called an omnibus. Englishman George Shillibeer brought the omnibus to London in 1829. Shillibeer's omnibus could carry almost two dozen people. In the 1920s, the first engine-powered double-decker buses appeared. The demand was great, and more and more companies began driving buses across London by the mid-1920s. One company, the London General Omnibus Company, wanted to make its buses stand out from the others. The company painted its buses bright red. Today, London's double-decker buses carry billions of passengers all around the city each year.

ANCIENT RUINS AT STONEHENGE

In Wiltshire, Sarah explores one of the United Kingdom's most iconic sites: Stonehenge.

The sarsen stones were arranged to line up with the sun's movement.

Built thousands of years ago on Wiltshire's Salisbury Plain, Stonehenge is a world-famous prehistoric monument. It is an enormous man-made circle of standing stones. Stonehenge consists of an outer ring of vertical standing stones called monoliths, many of which weigh approximately 25 tons (23 metric tons).[3] Horizontal stone crosspieces, called lintels, top the vertical monoliths. The vertical monoliths and lintels are made from chunks of sandstone called sarsen stones. Inside the outer ring, there is a smaller ring of bluestones. Today, the Stonehenge monument is incomplete, as many of the original stones have been broken up and taken away over the years.

Experts believe that human ancestors started working on the stone circle around 5,000 years ago in the late Neolithic Age. It took more than 1,000 years and several stages to build the monument. Archaeologists believe that Stonehenge's first builders began by using primitive tools to dig a large, circular ditch and bank, also called a henge. Deep pits within the circle, known as Aubrey holes after the man who discovered them in the 1600s, may have once held timber posts. Several hundred years later, builders placed bluestones into standing positions in a circular or horseshoe form. Builders also arranged sarsen stones in an outer ring. Some sarsens formed three-piece structures called trilithons in the monument's center. The largest sarsens weigh more than 40 tons (36 metric tons).[4] Archaeologists believe some of Stonehenge's stones came from hundreds of miles away. How the ancient builders moved these heavy stones over the long distance remains a mystery.

As Sarah walks around the stone monument, she wonders what Stonehenge was used for many centuries ago. She learns that although no one knows for sure, archaeologists have a few ideas. First, every year on the summer solstice in June—the longest day of the year—the sun rises over Stonehenge's Heel Stone. This is a large sarsen stone outside the main monument. Because of this, researchers suspect that Stonehenge may have served as a type of calendar. Some researchers suggest that the monument may have been a place of healing where the sick gathered in hopes of being cured. Others believe that the stone monument was a temple to the gods. Experts do know that Stonehenge was a burial place at some point, with an estimated 200 people buried on the grounds.[5]

After their visit to England's ancient monument, Sarah and her family drive back to London. As the sun sets over the River Thames, Sarah's mother urges her to get some rest because they have big plans for the next day. They will be taking a train to Manchester to watch a soccer match at

Fans pack the stands at Old Trafford stadium to see Manchester United soccer stars.

Old Trafford, the home of the Manchester United Football Club. It's sure to be another exciting experience in the United Kingdom.

THE UNITED KINGDOM: AN ISLAND COUNTRY

Visitors from around the world travel to the United Kingdom of Great Britain and Northern Ireland every year. From Scotland's craggy Highlands to the cosmopolitan city of London, the United Kingdom attracts people of all ages and interests. Known for its beautiful landscapes and rich history, the United Kingdom is a group of islands in the North Atlantic Ocean off the western coast of Europe. It is home to more than 67 million people, about a fifth of the population of the United States.[6]

The United Kingdom is made up of four countries: England, Wales, Scotland, and Northern Ireland. The first three are located on the island of Great Britain, while Northern Ireland is on the northernmost end of the island of Ireland. Numerous smaller islands are part of the United Kingdom too. These include the Isles of Scilly and the Isle of Wight off England's coast, the Orkney and Shetland Islands off Scotland's coast, and the island of Anglesey off the coast of Wales.

As the birthplace of the Industrial Revolution in the mid-1700s, the United Kingdom became the world's first industrialized country. During the peak of its power in the mid-1800s, the United Kingdom had taken control of approximately one-fourth of the world.[7] As the years went on and its colonies gained independence, the United Kingdom's influence lessened. Nevertheless, the United Kingdom remains one of the world's great powers with a rich heritage and promising future.

ONE COUNTRY OR FOUR?

Many people wonder if the United Kingdom is one country or four individual countries. The answer is both. The four countries of the United Kingdom—England, Scotland, Wales, and Northern Ireland—are individual countries. Each country has the ability to govern itself in certain matters, such as education and housing. The United Kingdom is also a sovereign state. That means it is represented by one centralized government that has authority over its members. In the United Kingdom, the Scottish, Welsh, and Northern Irish parliaments defer to the UK Parliament as the final authority in certain matters such as foreign policy.

CHAPTER **TWO**

GEOGRAPHY

The United Kingdom is well-known for its distinct and diverse landscapes. Across the nation are gently rolling plains and lush, green countryside. The United Kingdom also has coastal areas mixed with rocky moors and rough mountains. The landscapes in the country create a memorable picture.

Four major bodies of water surround the United Kingdom. The English Channel lies to the south of Great Britain and separates the United Kingdom from France on mainland Europe. To the west is the Atlantic Ocean. The Irish Sea flows between Great Britain and Ireland. The North Sea lies to the east of the British Isles, which are a group of islands that include Ireland, Great Britain, and smaller islands such as the Orkney Islands, the Isle of Man, and the Isles of Scilly.

The English countryside provides stunning views for anyone passing through.

MAP OF

THE UNITED KINGDOM

KEY:

- Capital
- City
- Point of Interest

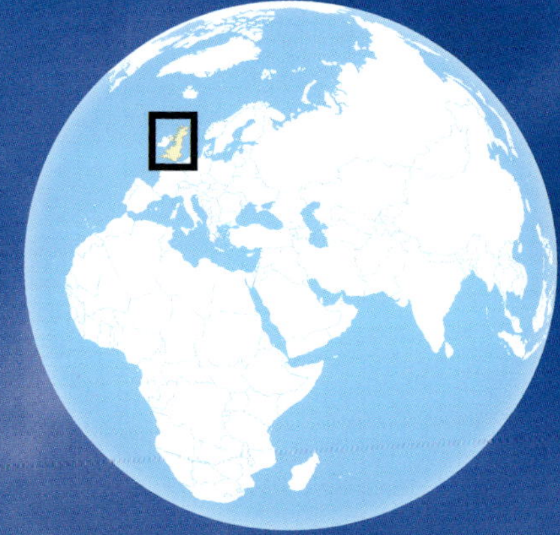

The United Kingdom is a relatively small country, with a land area of 93,410 square miles (241,930 sq km).[1] California is almost twice its size. The United Kingdom measures about 300 miles (480 km) from west to east at its widest point. From its northernmost tip in Scotland to England's southern coast, the United Kingdom stretches about 600 miles (965 km).[2]

In the United Kingdom, the sea is never far. It is no more than 75 miles (120 km) away from any point in the country.[3]

A DIVERSE LANDSCAPE

The United Kingdom has varied highland and lowland areas. The highland areas, also called uplands, sit high above sea level and often have mountains. Lowland areas are usually flat and not very high above sea level.

Many features of the United Kingdom's landscapes were formed over time in a process called glaciation. During the last Ice Age, about 20,000 years ago, ice sheets and glaciers covered large areas of the country. They shaped the land through processes such as erosion and weathering and created the landforms that remain today.

FROM MOUNTAINS TO GENTLY ROLLING HILLS

The landscape of the United Kingdom is diverse, from the mountains in Scotland to the gently rolling hills of England. In Scotland, visitors marvel at the country's mountainous peaks, spectacular cliffs, and rolling hills and plains. Scotland's landscapes can be separated into three main regions:

the Northern Highlands and Islands, the Southern Uplands, and the Central Lowlands. Scotland's Northern Highlands make up the country's northern half and have dramatic mountain ranges, including the Grampian Mountains and the Cairngorms. The mountains are divided by many broad valleys. In Scotland, the mountain Ben Nevis rises 4,413 feet (1,345 m) as the highest point in the United Kingdom.[4] Millions of years ago, Ben Nevis was an enormous active volcano that exploded and collapsed.

Not all of Scotland is mountainous. Along Scotland's border with England there are smooth, rolling hills. This region is known as the Southern Uplands. Many valleys and rivers cut through the moorlands in this area. Next to this region is Scotland's Central Lowlands. The Lowlands are an area of flatter land that stretches between the Northern Highlands and the hills of the Southern Uplands. Between the Lowlands and Highlands lies Scotland's largest lake by surface area, Loch Lomond. Scotland's largest city, Glasgow, and its capital city, Edinburgh, are in the Central Lowlands.

HIGHLAND BOUNDARY FAULT

The Highland Boundary Fault is a geological fault that stretches diagonally across Scotland from the west coast to the east. A fault is a fracture in Earth's crust. The Highland Boundary Fault separates Scotland's Highlands from its Lowlands. Around 400 million years ago, ancient continents collided, which created the fault. The mountains in the Highlands rose while the Lowlands sank, and a large valley formed across the middle of Scotland. The fault created both a geological division in Scotland and a cultural boundary between people living in the north and south.

Hiking in Northern Ireland's Mourne Mountains is a popular activity.

Mountains are an iconic part of the Welsh landscape. Some of them are the highest in the United Kingdom outside of Scotland. In the northwest, Snowdonia National Park is home to Wales's highest peak, Snowdon, at 3,560 feet (1,085 m).[5] The Brecon Beacons rise with felt-like green peaks, while the Cambrian Mountains feature rough stone peaks. Throughout the mountainous areas, rivers flow through valleys cut by glaciers long ago.

Flat plains and gently rolling hills fill most of England, creating the country's meadows and pastures. Many coastal areas are also low-lying, particularly in England's east and south. Some more prominent hills and mountainous regions can be found in northern England. The Pennines, a ridge of hills, runs down the center of northern England. The Cumbrian Mountains, including the Lake District, are a compact mountain region west of the northern Pennines. Deep gorges, narrow ridges, and sharp peaks can be found throughout the northern Cumbrian Mountains.

In Northern Ireland, gently rolling hills and low-lying plateaus are typical in many areas. In the southeast, the Mourne Mountains hold the highest point in Northern Ireland. This is Slieve Donard, and it rises to 2,796 feet (852 m).[6]

LAKES AND RIVERS

Numerous lakes and rivers can be found across the United Kingdom. When Ice Age glaciers melted, they formed the country's lakes. Many of the United Kingdom's lakes are long and narrow. Some are very deep. In each country, lakes have different names. In Scotland, lakes are called lochs. In Northern Ireland they are known as loughs, and they are called llyn in Wales. The United Kingdom's largest lake by area, Lough Neagh, is located in Northern Ireland and covers 153 square miles (396 sq km).[7] Located in the Scottish Highlands, Loch Ness is the United Kingdom's largest lake by volume. Officials say it holds more fresh water than all the lakes in England and Wales combined. Loch Ness is also famous worldwide for alleged sightings of Nessie, a mythical lake monster.

Several rivers flow through the United Kingdom's cities, towns, and countryside. They have an essential role in transporting goods and people, providing sources of water, generating hydroelectric power, and sustaining wildlife habitats. The United Kingdom's longest river is the

NESSIE, THE LOCH NESS MONSTER

Legend says that an ancient monster lives in the deepest regions of Scotland's Loch Ness. The first supposed sighting of the monster was reported in 564 CE. An Irish priest named Columba, who would later become St. Columba, said he spotted the monster while visiting Scotland. Since then, numerous people have reported seeing the mysterious monster that has been nicknamed Nessie. However, no scientific evidence has ever proven Nessie's existence.

River Severn at about 220 miles (354 km).[8] It begins in Wales and flows into the Atlantic Ocean near Bristol, England. The River Thames is the United Kingdom's second-longest river. It flows through Southern England and passes through several cities, including London, Reading, Windsor, and Oxford, before emptying into the North Sea.

COASTAL REGIONS

The United Kingdom has a lengthy coastline of 7,723 miles (12,429 km), including the coastlines of Great Britain, Northern Ireland, and its other islands.[9] A coastline is an area where the ocean meets land. Coastlines for the United Kingdom's islands are along the North Sea, Irish Sea, English Channel, and Atlantic Ocean. Bustling ports, scenic fishing harbors, sandy beaches, rocky shores, and stunning cliffs meet the sea at the land's edges.

The UK coastline is heavily indented along its length. These indentations or cuts result in the formation of inland bays, islets, gulfs, and peninsulas. Many of the coastline's indentations create good places for natural harbors.

CLIMATE IN THE BRITISH ISLES

Overall, the United Kingdom has a temperate climate with cool, wet winters and warm summers. The country rarely experiences extreme hot or cold weather. Temperatures are often between 59 and 63 degrees Fahrenheit (15 to 17°C) in the summer and 39 to 43 degrees Fahrenheit (4 to 6°C) in the winter.[10]

Within the United Kingdom, different regions have varying climates. For example, warm and dry summers and cold winters are typical in the southeast area. Winters in the southwest are mild but wet, and summers are warm and wet. In the northwest, mild winters and cool summers are typical, but rain is heavy year-round. And in the northeast regions, cold winters, cool summers, and steady rain year-round are typical.

Several factors affect the United Kingdom's climate, including ocean currents, air masses, and altitude. The North Atlantic current carries warm water from the South Atlantic Ocean to the United Kingdom's western coast. The winds moving from the southwest spread warmer conditions, creating milder winters in the western United Kingdom.

THE WHITE CLIFFS OF DOVER

In England, the White Cliffs of Dover are an iconic UK landmark. The white cliffs are made from chalk. The chalk layers formed from the skeletal remains of tiny green algae that lived in the ocean's upper levels. When the algae died, their remains sank to the ocean floor, where they combined with the remnants of other ocean organisms and formed chalk on the seabed. Over millions of years, the chalk layers built up. Slow changes in ocean and land levels caused the seabed to become exposed above sea level. The exposed chalk created the White Cliffs of Dover.

London gets the most rain during August and November.

Air masses can also affect the United Kingdom's climate. An air mass is a large amount of air that is mostly uniform in temperature and moisture. An air mass coming from polar regions and traveling over the Arctic Sea brings cold, wet weather to the United Kingdom. In contrast, an air mass traveling from the tropics over land brings hot and dry weather.

Altitude also affects climate in the United Kingdom. As warm, moist air moves over land, it rises over the United Kingdom's mountains. As the air rises, it cools. The moisture in the air condenses and falls to the ground as precipitation. As a result, there is typically higher rainfall in the United Kingdom's western upland regions than in lower-altitude regions in the east.

BIOME OF THE BRITISH ISLES

The United Kingdom's biome is classified as a temperate deciduous forest. A biome is a community of plants and animals that adapt to and live in a specific climate. Around the world, there are five major biomes: aquatic, grassland, forest, desert, and tundra. These major biomes can be divided further into freshwater, marine, savanna, tropical rain forest, temperate rain forest, and taiga.

Forest biomes are filled with trees. Forest biomes can exist at different latitudes around the world, which causes them to experience different climates. Temperate forests like those in the United Kingdom are in mid-latitudes. They experience four seasons and rainfall throughout the year. Deciduous forests have trees with broad leaves. These include oak and elm trees that drop their leaves in the fall. Temperate deciduous forest biomes are located in eastern North America, Western Europe, and some parts of East Asia.

Walking trails cut through forests in the United Kingdom. People walking along the trails can enjoy the country's natural settings.

CHAPTER **THREE**

PLANTS AND ANIMALS

More than 70,000 species of plants, animals, fungi, and other organisms live in the United Kingdom.[1] A variety of habitats across the land provide places for many of these creatures to thrive. A suitable habitat meets an organism's needs for survival. It includes food, water, shelter, and mates for animals to reproduce. A good habitat has the right amount of light, air, water, and soil for plants. The habitats in the United Kingdom include places such as woodland forests, moorlands, grasslands, fresh waters, coasts, rocky mountains, and more.

The United Kingdom has many geographical features that allow a variety of plant and animal species to thrive.

Woodlands give animals, such as tawny owls, places to live.

WOODLAND FORESTS

Much of the United Kingdom's land was once covered with woodland forests. Oak trees spread through the lowlands in the British Isles. Pine forests covered parts of Scotland, and birch forests were typical in the far north. Over centuries, humans have cleared many of the original woodland forests for lumber and farming. Now the remaining woodlands cover only about 10 percent of the United Kingdom, making it one of the least wooded countries in Europe.[2] The United Kingdom's most extensive remaining woodland forests are in northeastern Scotland, northwestern Wales, and eastern and southeastern England.

Across the United Kingdom, differences in climate and soil affect what types of trees and other plants grow. Oak trees grow most commonly in areas with more acidic soil, while ash trees grow in moist soil. Beech and yew trees

Moorlands are wild, open areas of land.

can thrive in thin, drought-prone soil, and birch trees grow in various conditions. Alder and willow trees can be found in wet conditions and river floodplains. Nutrient-poor soils in the uplands can support pine, spruce, and fir trees.

MOORLANDS AND HEATHLANDS

Moorlands and heathlands cover about one-fourth of UK land and are primarily found in the uplands of England.[3] Moorlands are found in high, hilly regions and have acidic, water-logged soil. Peat moss, heather, bilberry, and thin grasses grow in moorland areas of Scotland. Swampy moorlands have mosses, sedges, and small shrubs. The United Kingdom has approximately 75 percent of the world's moorlands.[4]

The United Kingdom's moorlands also serve as a natural reservoir for rain in the Highlands. The peat and moss in the moorlands soak up the rainwater, reducing flooding in nearby towns and villages. The moorlands release absorbed rainwater into rivers and streams, which can be used for various purposes. In addition, these areas reduce erosion. People can use moorlands for hunting game and hill farming.

Heathlands are broad, open areas with low-growing shrubs such as bilberry, gorse, and heather. Heathlands are unique because they were originally made by human agricultural and tree-clearing activities thousands of years ago. They occur on barren land that does not have nutrient-rich soil for farming. They have a few wet areas with acidic peat bogs and sphagnum moss. One-fifth of Earth's lowland heathland is in the United Kingdom.[5]

THE BAN ON FOX HUNTING

The sport of fox hunting has long been popular in the United Kingdom. Hunters follow trained dogs as they track, chase, and kill foxes. Several countries around the world have banned the practice because dogs dismember the hunted foxes and many people view this as cruel. In 2002, fox hunting was banned in Scotland. In 2004, England and Wales also banned the practice. Despite this, fox hunting still occurs in the United Kingdom as the existing bans are difficult to enforce.

ANIMALS IN THE UNITED KINGDOM

As an island nation, the United Kingdom has one of the longest coastlines in Europe. The UK coast features many habitats including cliffs, rocky shores, sand and shingle beaches, dunes, salt marshes, and

Male red deer have antlers that can weigh as much as 33 pounds (15 kg).

more. These coastal habitats are home to various plants and animals. The species that live in these habitats have adapted to survive in a salty environment.

Small mammals are common throughout the United Kingdom. Badgers, foxes, weasels, otters, and stoats are often spotted in the UK countryside. Rodents such as rats, squirrels, and mice, as well as insectivores such as hedgehogs, moles, and shrews, live in many areas across the country. Rabbits are also widespread across the United Kingdom. The brown hare lives in open lowlands,

The chaffinch has many different calls and a loud song. It's very common in Ireland and Great Britain.

while the mountain hare makes higher altitude lands like Scotland its home. The vole, a small rodent that eats grasses, is common on grassy moorlands. Voles attract predators such as the short-eared owl, hen harrier, turkey vulture, polecat, and European adder snake. The pine marten, a member of the weasel family, makes its home in the rocky moorlands.

Larger mammals are rarer in the United Kingdom. Several species have been hunted to extinction, including the boar, reindeer, and wolf. The red deer and roe deer are large mammals that still live in the United Kingdom. The red deer primarily lives in Scotland's Highlands and England's Exmoor Forest. The roe deer can be found in Scotland's woodlands and in southern England.

The United Kingdom is also home to several species of amphibians, including three species of newts and five species of frogs and toads.

Reptiles are less common in the country, with only three species of lizards and three species of snakes residing there, including the venomous adder. There are no snakes on the island of Ireland, including Northern Ireland.

HABITAT LOSS

Centuries of human activities such as farming, building, and industrial development have severely damaged UK habitats and the plants and animals that live in them. As a result, environmental experts warn that only half of the United Kingdom's natural biodiversity remains. Biodiversity is the range of species found in a habitat or place. When humans change the environment by clearing forests, planting fields, and building infrastructure, they damage biodiversity and reduce the number of species living in a place. These actions are causing the number of species to decline at a troubling rate. In fact, by 2020 the United Kingdom ranked in the bottom 10 percent of countries worldwide for remaining natural biodiversity.[6]

Many bird species are seen in the British Isles. The islands are part of a migration network. Some birds temporarily stop in the British Isles as they migrate between breeding and nonbreeding grounds. Hundreds of bird species live in the United Kingdom, and more than half of them are migratory. They live in different habitats across the country, including coastal regions, farmlands, and urban areas. Common birds include the sparrow, starling, chaffinch, and blackbird. Some people enjoy watching for these birds. Common game birds in the country include wild pigeons, grouse, and pheasant.

The United Kingdom's many freshwater rivers and lakes provide habitats for various fish, including salmon, trout, perch, pike, grayling, and roach. However, pollution has caused the populations of some of these freshwater fish species to decline. The seas near the United Kingdom are fertile habitats for several species, including cod, haddock, whiting, mackerel, coalfish, herring, turbot, and plaice.

Arachnids and insects such as money spiders, moths, ground and rove beetles, and crane flies are common in the moorlands. Insects, including beetles and moths, are part of the diet of moorland birds. Butterflies such as the mountain ringlet, small heath, and large heath are common in the moorlands too. Other moorland insects include bumblebees and several species of dragonflies.

FOXES IN THE CITY

Foxes are increasingly appearing in urban areas across the United Kingdom. In England alone, there are about 150,000 urban foxes. That is the equivalent of about one fox for every 300 people. While the total number of foxes in the United Kingdom has dropped 42 percent since 1995, the number living in urban areas has quadrupled.[8] The loss of prey in rural areas due to disease, hunting, and pesticide use is driving foxes to search for food in new places. In addition, the growth of urban areas brings cities closer to fox populations.

THREATENED SPECIES

In 2020, scientists warned that 25 percent of the United Kingdom's native mammals were "at imminent risk of extinction."[7] They named 11 mammals to the country's first official Red List of endangered species, including the wildcat, red squirrel, water vole, hazel dormouse, and hedgehog. Another five mammals, including the mountain hare, were deemed near threatened, which meant they may soon face a threat of extinction. Another report from October 2019 found that populations of the United Kingdom's most important animal species, such as hedgehogs, bats, and hares, had declined by an average of 60 percent since 1970.[9]

Scientists point to the destruction of natural habitats, the introduction of invasive species, and persecution as the main threats to the United Kingdom's wildlife. Historical persecution, or killing a specific group of animals, has endangered animals such as wildcats and beavers. Other species have declined because of diseases. For instance, the red squirrel is impacted by a disease introduced by grey squirrels, a species that is not native to the United Kingdom. And other species have struggled to survive because of the loss of suitable habitats. For example, the destruction of riverside habitats has harmed water voles.

Since the 1500s, more than 130 animal species have gone extinct in the United Kingdom.[10] This includes large mammals such as wolves and lynx and smaller animals such as the apple bumblebee and the common tree frog.

Although these animals are endangered, there is still hope that their populations can recover. Tony Juniper is the chair of Natural England, an environmental advisory agency. Juniper notes that the 2020 report on endangered species is a wake-up call to the country. It highlights the critical work ecological groups are doing to recover and restore the United Kingdom's animal and plant populations.

CHAPTER **FOUR**

HISTORY

The United Kingdom has a long, rich history. According to archaeologists, the earliest humans to arrive in the area that would become the United Kingdom came to the region about 900,000 years ago. These people periodically traveled to the area during warm periods between Ice Ages. At the time, the United Kingdom was a peninsula of Europe and was connected to the European continent. The oldest human remains in the United Kingdom date back to about 500,000 years ago and belong to a six-foot (1.8 m) tall man. Archaeologists have also uncovered evidence of Neanderthals living in the area between 300,000 and 35,000 years ago. Later, the direct ancestors of modern humans arrived.

The earliest humans in the United Kingdom survived by hunting animals and gathering food items

At the British Museum in London, visitors learn about various historical periods.

such as nuts and berries and other resources they needed. Most lived nomadic lifestyles and traveled from place to place searching for food. Around 6500 BCE, rising oceans covered the land connecting Great Britain and Europe, causing Great Britain to become an island.

ANCIENT BRITAIN

Between 5000 BCE and 4500 BCE, farming was introduced in the area. People who traveled to the island from continental Europe by boat brought farming techniques. These early people often farmed barley, wheat, and pulses—a type of legume crop. They still depended on gathering wild plants, animals, and other resources.

During this period, new monuments appeared. Among them were timber circles, such as Woodhenge, which cropped up around 2300 BCE near Salisbury. Earth mounds such as Silbury Hill near Avebury are estimated to have been created around 2400 BCE. Early people also built stone circles and earthwork henges. They created a combination of henges and circles in some places, such as Stonehenge.

COMING TO THE ISLANDS

Throughout history, many different people have arrived on the shores of the United Kingdom. Sometime around 1000 BCE, the Celtic people landed on Great Britain and Ireland from central and eastern Europe. The Celts were a collection of tribes that shared similar languages, religions, and cultural practices. They were known as fierce warriors. Many Celtic people lived in roundhouses.

Historians today still don't know what purpose Silbury Hill served for those who built it.

A roundhouse's walls were often made from local materials such as wattle and daub, a material created by sticks and twigs covered with mud or clay. The roofs were shaped like cones and thatched with straw or heather.

Around 55 to 54 BCE, Roman forces led by Julius Caesar invaded the British Isles. Caesar later made peace with the tribes living there and returned to Europe. Nearly 100 years later, the Roman emperor Claudius launched another invasion of Great Britain in 43 CE. The Roman invaders remained there for almost four centuries. They built roads, bathhouses, sewers, and large villas. In the early 300s, Christianity spread across the Roman Empire, including Great Britain. England and Wales remained part of the Roman Empire until the 400s.

After the Romans withdrew, the Angles, Saxons, and Jutes from northern Germany arrived and settled throughout England. Those living in England became known as Anglo-Saxons. Several Anglo-Saxon kingdoms were established, while Celtic tribes remained in Wales and Scotland. In the 700s, Viking raiders from northern Europe arrived on England's coasts. In the late 800s and 900s, the Anglo-Saxon people defeated the Vikings and established a united English kingdom.

The Romans began building Hadrian's Wall in 122 CE. This was a defensive barrier that stretched across northern Great Britain.

In 1066, the death of the English ruler, Edward the Confessor, sparked a disagreement about who should be England's next leader. A Saxon king, Harold II, claimed the English throne. But France's Duke of Normandy, William, launched an invasion of England. At the Battle of Hastings in 1066, William defeated Harold II. His victory brought feudalism to England.

MONARCHY REIGNS

For centuries, kings and queens ruled over England. The Tudor monarchs (1485–1603) were among the most influential. King Henry VIII ruled between 1509 and 1547. He had six wives and ordered two of them to be beheaded. Henry VIII also broke with the Roman Catholic Church and established the Church of England.

Henry's daughter Elizabeth I became one of the greatest Tudor monarchs. She ruled between 1558 and 1603. Elizabeth I led England to military victory over Spain, the country's greatest rival at the time. When Elizabeth I died without an heir, the Tudor dynasty ended. The English throne passed to James VI of Scotland. Once on the English throne, he became known as James I of England and launched the Stuart dynasty.

FEUDALISM

Feudalism was a common practice in medieval Europe between the 800s and the 1400s. In a feudal system, a lord or noble owned land and granted possession of the land to a vassal. The lord also protected the vassal. In exchange, the vassal provided some service to the lord. In England, the king owned the land. Below the king, a vassal, often a baron or knight, held the land on behalf of the king. Serfs, or peasants, did most of the work on the land and supported the upper classes.

James I ruled from 1603 to 1625. His rise to the throne brought Scotland and England together, and he became the first king to rule both countries simultaneously. His successor, Charles I, was executed, and then Parliament declared England a republic. The English monarchy returned in 1660 when Charles II, the son of Charles I, was asked to take the throne. The last of the Stuart monarchs, Queen Anne, died in 1714 without leaving an heir.

After Queen Anne's death, the German Hanoverians succeeded her. This began the Georgian age in England, as the first four Hanover kings were named George. During this time, Great Britain's empire continued to expand its reach. In 1788, Great Britain began colonizing new areas in Australia. The empire also saw growth in Upper Canada, which is known today as Ontario. As the Industrial Revolution dawned, Great Britain became the world's first industrialized nation.

In 1837, Queen Victoria was crowned. She ruled Britain for more than 60 years. During her long reign, Britain grew in wealth and influence. The British Empire continued to take over more countries and reached the peak of its power.

The Victorian era ended in the 1900s as the House of Windsor took over the monarchy. King George V, who ruled from 1910 to 1936, passed the throne to his oldest son, Edward VIII. But Edward gave up his power to marry an American woman named Wallis Simpson. His younger brother, George VI, became king in 1936 and held the title until he died in 1952. George VI's daughter Elizabeth II became the United Kingdom's queen upon his death. Queen Elizabeth II remained a steady constant in the British monarchy for decades. In 2022, she celebrated her seventieth year as the queen. She died in September 2022.

The British Royal Navy often dominated conflicts at sea due to its well-designed ships and highly trained crews.

EXPANSION OF THE BRITISH EMPIRE

In the 1500s, Great Britain began to expand its control into other parts of the world. In 1588, the British Royal Navy defeated the Spanish Armada and became the world's dominant naval power. Britain colonized areas in Asia, Africa, and the Americas. Britain and its colonies became known as the British Empire. In the early 1800s, the United Kingdom defeated France in the Napoleonic Wars (1801–1815) and became Europe's most powerful country.

By the 1800s, the United Kingdom was also one of the world's wealthiest countries. Trade with other countries generated enormous wealth for the British Empire. By the early 1900s, the British

Empire ruled more than one-fourth of the world's land area.

AMERICAN REVOLUTION

In the early 1600s, Great Britain began colonizing North America. In 1775, colonists there declared their independence from Great Britain. The conflict turned into a war known as the American Revolution (1775–1783). The war officially ended when the Treaty of Paris was signed in 1783 by representatives of King George III and the American colonists. The American colonies formed a new country, the United States of America.

FORMATION OF THE UNITED KINGDOM

The four countries in the United Kingdom—England, Scotland, Wales, and Northern Ireland—started as independent nations. Over many years and battles, they eventually joined together to form today's United Kingdom. In the late 1200s, England conquered Wales, which was still a group of separate Celtic kingdoms. But the countries weren't officially united until 1536.

At first, England and Scotland were rival kingdoms that fought many battles, as Scotland wanted to remain independent. However, in 1603 Scotland and England were united under King James I. In 1707, the parliaments of the two countries were joined. The union of England, Scotland, and Wales became the kingdom of Great Britain.

Like Scotland, Ireland did not want to be ruled by England. By the late 1600s, however, England had gained control of Ireland. In 1801, Ireland was officially joined with England, Scotland, and Wales. The four nations became the United Kingdom of Great Britain and Ireland, also called the United Kingdom.

IRISH INDEPENDENCE

Many Irish people were not happy living under British rule and wanted their independence. In 1921, most of Ireland broke away from the United Kingdom and formed the Irish Free State, which later became the Republic of Ireland. However, several northern regions of Ireland, today's Northern Ireland, remained part of the United Kingdom.

Some Irish people were unhappy about Ireland splitting into two parts, with Northern Ireland remaining under British control. People protested British influence in Ireland. This led to a decades-long conflict that finally ended in 1998.

THE TROUBLES

The Troubles was a period of 30 years of conflict over Northern Ireland. The Unionists wanted Northern Ireland to remain part of the United Kingdom. The Nationalists wanted Northern Ireland to become part of the Republic of Ireland. The conflict was often violent. Terrorism from multiple sides led to more than 3,600 deaths and tens of thousands of injuries.[1] An agreement made on Good Friday, April 10, 1998, ended the violence. The Good Friday Agreement was a compromise that established relationships between the United Kingdom, Northern Ireland, and the Republic of Ireland. It also established the Northern Ireland Assembly, which brought the two sides together to handle local matters.

WORLD WARS

The 1900s brought two world wars, and the United Kingdom played a key role in both. In 1914, the murder of Archduke Franz Ferdinand of Austria sparked a series of conflicts in Europe that triggered World War I (1914–1918). The United Kingdom joined with the Allied powers of France, Russia, Italy, Japan, and eventually the United States against the

Central powers of Germany, Austria-Hungary, and Turkey. The war ended in 1918 with the defeat of Germany and the Central powers.

Peace across Europe, however, would not last for long. In 1939, Germany, led by ruler Adolf Hitler and his Nazi Party, invaded Poland. The United Kingdom and France were allies of Poland and had promised to defend it. Within days, the United Kingdom and France declared war on Germany. World War II (1939–1945) had begun. Many countries eventually joined the war. The United Kingdom, France, the United States, and the Soviet Union were among the countries fighting on one side as the Allied powers. Together, they fought the Axis powers of Germany, Italy, and Japan.

By 1940, Germany had conquered much of Europe and prepared to invade the United Kingdom. During the summer and fall of 1940, the British Royal Air Force (RAF) battled the German air force, the Luftwaffe, in the Battle of Britain. In September 1940, the Germans began to attack London. For several weeks, they carried out heavy bombing raids. However, the RAF was eventually able to push back the Luftwaffe attacks. At the end of October, the Battle of Britain ended. Germany failed to control the skies over Britain. However, Germany's night bombings of London and other British cities continued until May 1941.

In World War II, 70,000 UK civilians died, primarily due to German bombing raids.[2]

The war continued in Europe and the Pacific for several more years. Eventually, the fighting ended in 1945. In May of that year, German forces surrendered to the Allies in Europe. A few months later, in September 1945, Japan surrendered in the Pacific.

A CHANGING WORLD

World War II had a significant impact around the globe. London and other cities across Great Britain had sustained heavy damage by the war's end. The United Kingdom spent many years rebuilding its cities, infrastructure, and economy. At the same time, the colonies were becoming expensive to maintain, and many of them, including those in Africa and Asia, wanted to be free of British rule. UK colonies around the world eventually got their independence.

At home, the people of Northern Ireland, Wales, and Scotland also struggled for more independence and self-rule. In the 1990s, the United Kingdom granted additional governing powers to new parliaments in Wales, Scotland, and Northern Ireland. The UK parliament in London, however, continued to govern the entire United Kingdom. In some UK countries, movements to gain independence continued into the new millennium.

In 1973, the country joined the European Union (EU). The EU is a political and economic alliance of European countries. It was formed to improve and strengthen economic and political cooperation in Europe after World War II. The EU requires its members to follow specific laws about trade, security, immigration, and environmental regulations. However, some people in the United Kingdom did not approve of the EU's laws. In 2016, the United Kingdom voted to leave the EU, a

After World War II, the United Kingdom began rebuilding cities, such as London, that had been damaged by Nazi bombs.

move that was known as Brexit. After a transition period, the United Kingdom officially left the EU in January 2020.

CHAPTER **FIVE**

PEOPLE AND CULTURE

Various influences have shaped the people and cultures of the United Kingdom. Different groups have brought their unique traditions and left their imprints on the British Isles. For centuries, people have migrated to the United Kingdom from many places around the world. Some arrived on the country's shores to escape political or religious persecution. Some migrants traveled to the United Kingdom in hopes of escaping poverty and creating a better life for themselves and their families. They joined the people already living in the United Kingdom whose ancestors had arrived with the Celts, Angles, Saxons, Jutes, Danes, and Normans.

St. Patrick's Day is an important holiday for people in Northern Ireland.

Many Jewish people arrived in the United Kingdom between the late 1800s and the 1930s. After World War II, some European refugees who had lost their homes resettled in the United Kingdom. Some people from former UK colonies in Africa, the Caribbean, and Asia came to the United Kingdom for work. And large immigrant groups from the West Indies and South Asia began to arrive in the 1950s and 1960s. Immigrants from other European nations, Latin America, Southeast Asia, Sri Lanka, India, Pakistan, and Bangladesh have made the United Kingdom their home too.

By 2011, the population of the United Kingdom was primarily made up of Caucasian people, at 86 percent. Another main ethnic group living in the United Kingdom included Asians, at 7.5 percent. Black people made up 3.3 percent of the UK population, and mixed or other ethnic groups were at 3.2 percent.[1]

SCOTLAND'S CLANS

In Scotland, clans are kinship groups of people who share a sense of identity and history. Clan members traditionally lived in the same region. Each clan had a leader or chief. Not all clan members were related to the chief. Many were invited to join the clan to create an alliance or gain protection. For centuries, clans controlled Scotland's political system. This lasted until the defeat of the Scots by the British in 1746. Today, Scotland has hundreds of clans. Many still host social events to continue their traditions.

LANGUAGE

The primary language of the United Kingdom is English, although the accent, pronunciation, and spelling of British English can differ from American English. In addition to English, other native

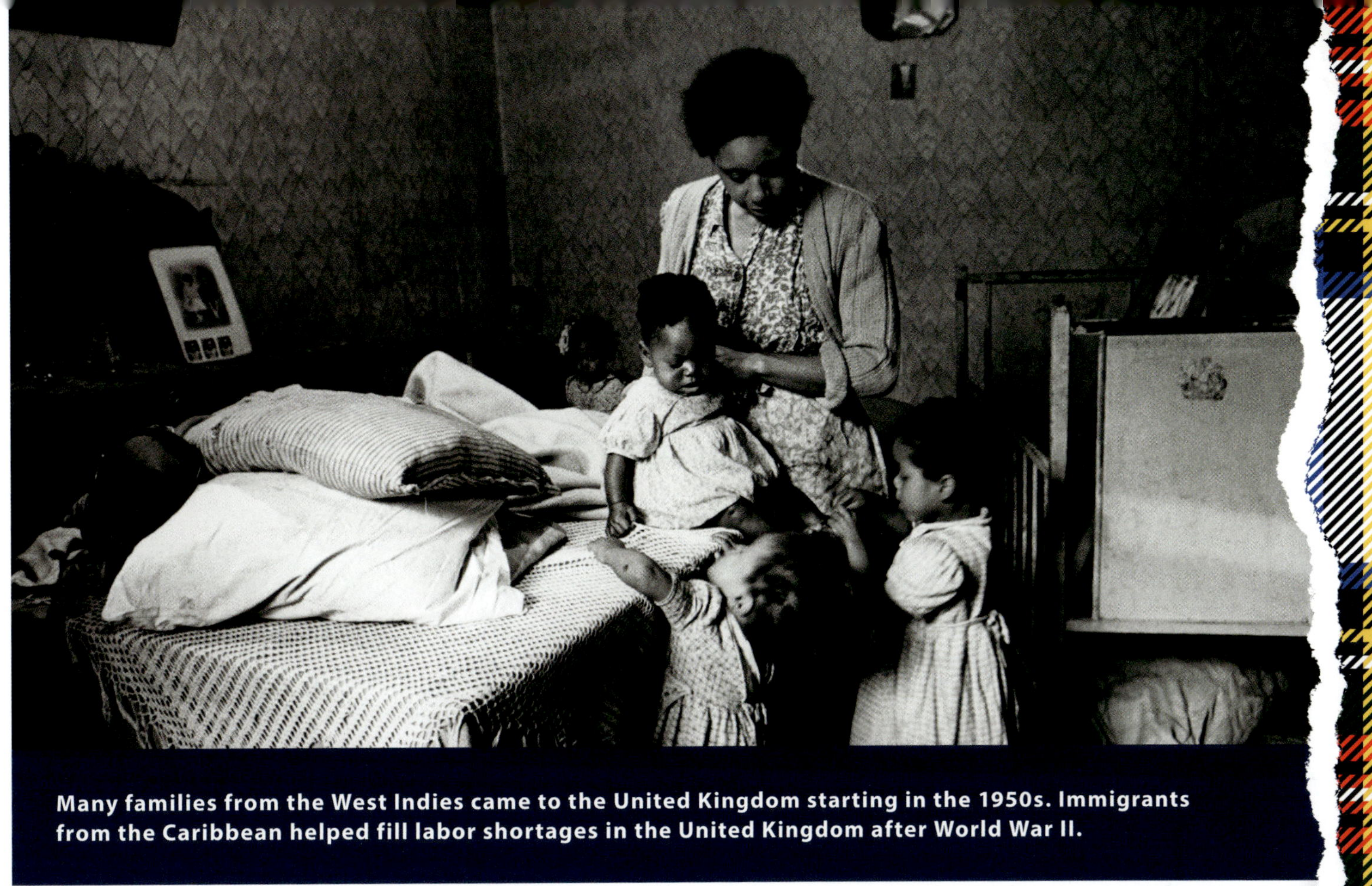

Many families from the West Indies came to the United Kingdom starting in the 1950s. Immigrants from the Caribbean helped fill labor shortages in the United Kingdom after World War II.

languages are spoken in the country. Travelers may hear Cornish in Cornwall, Welsh in Wales, Gaelic and Scots in Scotland, and Ulster Scots and Irish in Northern Ireland. These native languages came from a common European origin. However, over time they developed and split into different languages in the British Isles, and each language has its own grammar and vocabulary. The surviving native languages are most commonly used in rural areas. In some schools, youth learn them as a second language.

Liverpool Cathedral is the largest church in Great Britain. It occupies approximately 104,275 square feet (9,687 sq m).

Immigrants, international students, and visitors have brought a rich linguistic diversity to the British Isles. In London, a person may hear more than 300 languages being used. It is a mark of the area's rich cultures.[2]

RELIGION

Christianity is the most popular religion in the United Kingdom. Several branches of Christianity are practiced, including Anglican, Presbyterian, Methodist, and Roman Catholic. The different Christian denominations developed from centuries-old divisions in the church. One of the biggest divisions occurred during the 1500s in England when King Henry VIII disputed the authority of the Roman Catholic pope. The pope is the head of the Catholic Church, but King Henry VIII wanted to be in charge. This separation from Rome led to Henry VIII's founding of the Church of England, an Anglican church that remains the state church in England today.

In Scotland, the Reformation, a religious revolution in the 1500s, led to the establishment of the Church of Scotland. The new church formed local groups of ministers and elders to govern the church instead of the bishops who governed the Church of England. While these religious divisions occurred in England and Scotland, Protestantism has remained the predominant religion in Northern

THE SCOTTISH KILT

Scottish kilts are pleated, knee-length skirts that Scottish men have worn since the 1500s. Originally called the Feileadh Mor in Scotland, they also include long, thick pieces of fabric draped over the shoulders. At first, the Feileadh Mor was designed to protect the wearer from the stormy Scottish weather. In the early 1800s, the kilt evolved into a symbol of Scottish identity and became part of traditional Scottish dress. Today, Scottish kilts are worn as a symbol of pride and to celebrate Celtic heritage.

Ireland. Over the following centuries, more Protestant denominations emerged in the United Kingdom, including the Methodist Church.

Other religions are also practiced in the United Kingdom. The country is home to the second-largest Jewish community in Western Europe. Jehovah's Witnesses, Mormons, Muslims, and Hindus have active communities. Immigrants have also established community religious centers, including those for members of the Greek and Russian Orthodox churches and the Armenian Church.

Citizens and residents of the United Kingdom enjoy religious freedom and can practice whatever religion they choose. All churches and religious communities may own property and operate schools. In addition, there are many nonreligious people in the United Kingdom. In 2019, more than half of the people in the country said they weren't part of a religious institution.[3]

CULTURE AND THE ARTS

UK culture has been influenced by the traditions of England, Wales, Scotland, Northern Ireland, and the colonies of the British Empire. Arts in the United Kingdom have made an impact worldwide with numerous contributions in literature, theater, music, and more. Famous

Only Protestants, such as Queen Elizabeth II, *right*, may become kings or queens of the United Kingdom.

writers from all corners of the United Kingdom have written enduring pieces of literature enjoyed around the globe. Some well-known British novelists include Jane Austen, Charles Dickens, Thomas Hardy, and Mary Shelley. Lewis Carroll gained fame for his children's books, *Alice's Adventures in Wonderland* and *Through the Looking-Glass*. Sir Arthur Conan Doyle created the fictional detective Sherlock Holmes, while J. R. R. Tolkien created fantasy tales such as *The Hobbit* and the Lord of the Rings trilogy. Neil Gaiman has created popular comics and novels.

The United Kingdom has also produced many famous poets, including William Wordsworth, Lord Byron, and John Keats. Victorian-era poets include Elizabeth Barrett Browning, Robert Browning, and Alfred Tennyson. British playwrights, directors, and actors have brightened stages and screens worldwide. One of the world's most famous poets and playwrights, William Shakespeare, wrote dozens of plays that are still performed today. Actors such as Kate Winslet, Idris Elba, Tom Holland, Gemma Chan, Dev Patel, Riz Ahmed, and Jessica Henwick have enthralled audiences with their work.

British composers and musicians have created music that entertains listeners worldwide. The Beatles, one of the most famous British pop music groups, swept the world in the mid-1960s. Other British musicians include Ed Sheeran, Adele, Elton John, Dua Lipa, and Estelle.

CULTURAL INSTITUTIONS

The United Kingdom is home to many museums and other cultural institutions. The British Museum in London holds artifacts from around the world. Other London museums display

MINI **BIO**

WILLIAM SHAKESPEARE

William Shakespeare was born in 1564 in Stratford-upon-Avon, England. His father was a successful businessman and civic figure in town. At age 18, Shakespeare married 26-year-old Anne Hathaway. They had three children, Susanna, Hamnet, and Judith. There is little information about the early years of Shakespeare's life, but it is believed he spent much of his time writing and performing plays in London.

In London, Shakespeare became a founding member of the Lord Chamberlain's Men, an acting company. He produced an average of two plays a year with the company. With the support of King James I, the company renamed itself the King's Men. During this time, Shakespeare wrote some of his most famous plays, such as *King Lear*, *Macbeth*, and *The Tempest*. Around 1613, Shakespeare retired. He died three years later. Over his career, he wrote 38 plays, two narrative poems, 154 sonnets, and several other works.[4] His plays remain popular today and are studied and performed on stage and in film worldwide. His writings have also been published in various forms. Though centuries have passed since his death, Shakespeare remains one of the most important figures in world literature.

Many scholars of literature consider William Shakespeare to be the most skillful dramatist to ever live.

famous pieces of art, sculptures, and historical artifacts, including the National Gallery, the Tate galleries, the Imperial War Museum, the National Portrait Gallery, and the Victoria and Albert Museum.

Outside of London, there are many other libraries, museums, and institutions. The National Museum of Scotland; the Writers' Museum in Edinburgh, Scotland; the National Museum of Wales in Cardiff, Wales; and the Ulster Museum in Belfast, Northern Ireland, preserve the art, history, and culture of the United Kingdom. People visit these places to learn about the country's long history and diverse background.

SPORTS AND RECREATION

Several sports can trace their competitive beginnings to the United Kingdom. The modern game of soccer, called football in Europe, is generally thought to have started in England. Soccer's first competitive organization, the Football Association, was founded in 1863 in England. In 1872, a soccer rivalry between Scotland and England began. The first match between the two nations took place in Glasgow that year.

Today, the United Kingdom has numerous soccer teams and leagues, including famous English clubs such as Manchester United, Arsenal, and Liverpool FC. In Scotland, fans cheer for teams such as Glasgow's Celtic and Rangers clubs. Scotland and England regularly send national teams to compete in international tournaments such as the World Cup. Wales and Northern Ireland also have national soccer leagues.

Other popular sports such as rugby and cricket got their starts in the United Kingdom too. Rugby was first played around 1823 at the Rugby School in England. Today, England, Scotland, and Wales have rugby club competitions and leagues. They also send national rugby teams to international competitions, including the Six Nations Championship and World Cup tournaments.

Cricket may have been first played in the 1200s in England. By the 1800s, English counties organized formal competitions. International competitions, called tests, started in 1877 with a match between England and Australia.

In addition to UK sports, British athletes are regular competitors at the Olympic Games. The United Kingdom has competed in every modern Olympics, which began in 1896, and the country has even hosted the Olympics three times, in 1908, 1948, and 2012 in London. Over the years, UK athletes have won many Olympic medals and have had strong performances in tennis, rowing, yachting, and figure skating.

British cyclist Jason Kenny is the United Kingdom's most decorated Olympian, winning seven gold medals and nine medals in total.

The United Kingdom is well-known for its golf courses. Golf enthusiasts worldwide travel to the beautiful courses in Ireland and Scotland to play a round of 18 holes. The United Kingdom hosts the Open Championship, also known as the British Open. This is one of golf's four major annual tournaments. The Open is often held at Scotland's world-famous St. Andrews golf course.

Every summer, the United Kingdom hosts the All-England Championships, also called Wimbledon. This is a tennis competition for the world's best players. Annual horse-racing events in the country, such as the Royal Ascot, the Derby, and the Grand National steeplechase, are also popular.

FOOD

English food traditionally features beef, lamb, pork, and chicken. It is often prepared plainly and served with potatoes. Fish such as cod or haddock are deep-fried in batter and served with fried potato slices. This makes up the country's legendary dish known as fish-and-chips. Traditionally, take-out fish-and-chips are wrapped in old newspapers to keep them warm on the way home. Roast beef, Yorkshire pudding, and steak and kidney pie are also popular English dishes.

In Wales, one might eat cawl, which is a stew, and bara brith, which is a currant cake. In Scotland, the national dish is haggis. This is made from ground sheep entrails mixed with spices and oats, tied and cooked in a sheep's stomach. In Northern Ireland, Irish stew, homemade tarts, and small meat pies called pasties are popular.

PUB LIFE

The neighborhood pub is a central part of UK culture. It is much more than a place to get a drink. It is also a hub for social interaction and is often the center of community life in villages, towns, and cities. People choose a favorite pub based on location, the availability of a specific drink, food, atmosphere, and the presence of friends. People gather with friends to share a drink, engage in conversation, cheer on the local soccer team, and play a few games of darts or snooker.

Haggis is often served with mashed potatoes, which the British call mash.

CHAPTER **SIX**

POLITICS

The United Kingdom's system of government has developed over many centuries. Kings and queens once ruled over the British Empire and took advice from a council of religious leaders and nobles. Over time, this council of advisers expanded to become Parliament, which passes all of the country's laws today.

The English people believed God blessed the king and gave him the right to rule over them. They also thought that the king's successor, usually his oldest son, inherited the right to rule. For many years, the king was the country's sole lawmaker. He had so much power that he could often break his own laws with no one able to hold him accountable.

In 1215, England's King John lost a war against powerful barons, and they forced him to sign the

The UK monarch typically opens every new Parliament session, as Queen Elizabeth II did in 2021.

Magna Carta. This was a document that guaranteed certain rights to the barons. The Magna Carta also stated that the king must obey the country's laws. After the Magna Carta, the king increasingly sought the advice of ministers and nobles to approve his policies and projects.

Today, the UK government is made up of the monarch and three branches of government. The legislative branch debates and passes laws. The executive branch carries out the laws and manages the government, and the judicial branch enforces the laws.

BILL OF RIGHTS 1689

The English Bill of Rights was signed into law in 1689 by King William III and Queen Mary II, who were corulers of England. The Bill of Rights guarantees several constitutional and civic rights to British citizens and gives Parliament power over the monarchy. One of the core ideas in the English Bill of Rights was that the monarch could not tax subjects without the consent of their representatives in Parliament. This concept would later spark a dispute with the American colonies, which were being taxed by the king but did not have representation in Parliament.

A CONSTITUTIONAL MONARCHY

The United Kingdom is a constitutional monarchy. In this form of government, a sovereign—a king or queen—is the head of state but does not rule the country. Instead, the power to make and pass legislation belongs to an elected Parliament. As the head of state, the sovereign does not vote or run for election and is expected to remain neutral in all political matters. After Queen Elizabeth II's death in 2022, her oldest son became King Charles III.

MINI **BIO**

QUEEN ELIZABETH II

Elizabeth Alexandra Mary was born on April 21, 1926. Her grandfather was King George V and her father was the Duke of York. As a child, Elizabeth enjoyed riding horses at her family's country home. While Elizabeth was part of the royal family, she did not expect to become queen. That changed for her in 1936 when King George V died. Her father's older brother, Edward, renounced the throne and Elizabeth's father unexpectedly became king. Suddenly, ten-year-old Elizabeth was next in line to the crown. Even at a young age, she prepared to be the future queen and showed a strong sense of duty.

As a teenager, Elizabeth met Prince Philip of Greece and Denmark. In 1947, Elizabeth and Philip announced their engagement and wed in Westminster Abbey. The couple had four children: Charles, Anne, Andrew, and Edward. On February 6, 1952, her father King George VI died and 25-year-old Elizabeth became queen of the United Kingdom. Queen Elizabeth II's reign extended longer than any British monarch in history. She died on September 8, 2022, at age 96. While the world underwent many changes during her reign, the queen remained a steadfast and memorable monarch.

In 2015, Queen Elizabeth II officially became the longest-reigning monarch in UK history, exceeding Queen Victoria, who ruled in the late 1800s.

Although kings and queens do not have political roles, they do perform important duties on behalf of the country. They participate in several ceremonial and formal roles in the UK government. The sovereign formally opens and closes each session of Parliament and gives royal assent to bills passed by that body, which signals they have become law. The sovereign approves orders and proclamations made by the Privy Council, an advisory body to the monarch. The monarch also meets regularly with the UK prime minister and has formal roles with assemblies based in Scotland, Wales, and Northern Ireland.

A PARLIAMENTARY DEMOCRACY

The United Kingdom is also a parliamentary democracy. UK citizens elect representatives to Parliament, the country's legislative body, to represent their interests and carry out their wishes. Parliament is responsible for passing laws and authorizing taxes and government budgets.

COMMONWEALTH REALMS

Beyond the United Kingdom, the monarch's reign reaches more than a dozen countries. These countries are called commonwealth realms. They are former colonies of the British Empire that cooperate with other member countries and maintain friendly relations. While they recognize the UK monarch as their head of state, they are independent sovereign states. The commonwealth realms include Antigua and Barbuda, Australia, the Bahamas, Belize, Canada, Grenada, Jamaica, New Zealand, Papua New Guinea, Saint Kitts and Nevis, Saint Lucia, Saint Vincent and the Grenadines, Solomon Islands, and Tuvalu. However, several realms have discussed becoming republics and no longer recognizing the UK monarch as head of state.

Parliament also oversees the work of the UK government and debates current issues. Parliament is made of two Houses: the House of Lords and the House of Commons. The two Houses of Parliament work together on behalf of UK citizens.

The House of Lords is Parliament's upper house. It does not have a set number of members, and in 2022 approximately 800 people were part of the House.[1] The members are called Lords or peers. Members of the House of Lords are not elected. Some Lords, called spiritual peers, are bishops of the Church of England, such as the archbishops of York and Canterbury. Other peers are members of the nobility or members who inherited their seats from their families and hold them for life. Others are appointed as Lords by the sovereign on the prime minister's recommendation because they are experts in their fields. Once appointed, these members hold their seats for life. Over time, the powers of the House of Lords have gradually declined. Today, the House of Lords allows people from a wide range of backgrounds to discuss and review government policies.

The House of Commons is Parliament's lower house and has 650 elected members, called members of Parliament (MPs).[2] MPs are elected by popular vote of British citizens aged 18 and older. The House of Commons was created in the 1200s when representatives from UK towns traveled to Parliament to air their grievances. Eventually, they formed their own House to participate in the UK government. Over time, the House of Commons has become more powerful and is an essential governing body today.

Most proposed laws, called bills, can be introduced in either the House of Commons or the House of Lords. Bills related to finance or representation can be introduced only in the House of

MPs debate bills and answer questions in the House of Commons.

Commons. When a new bill is introduced to the House of Commons, members debate it before sending it to a committee, where more in-depth debate occurs and potential amendments are discussed. When the bill returns to the House of Commons, members vote on it. If the bill passes, it moves over to the House of Lords. Members of the House of Lords review the bill and propose amendments if necessary. The House of Lords can also propose and pass its own bills, which are then sent to the House of Commons for passage.

Parliament also controls government finances and oversees government operations. It reviews and debates the country's proposed budget and approves government spending. Committees within Parliament oversee various government departments to make sure they operate efficiently and effectively. Every week, members of the House of Commons and the House of Lords ask government ministers questions about the running of their government departments. The House of Lords also holds debates on current issues of importance to the United Kingdom.

THE EXECUTIVE BRANCH AND THE PRIME MINISTER

The prime minister leads the executive branch of the UK government. The prime minister is traditionally the leader of Parliament's majority party and is formally appointed by the sovereign.

Boris Johnson was the UK prime minister from 2019 to 2022.

The prime minister is responsible for the policies and decisions of the UK government. He or she appoints other government officials, oversees government agencies, and has meetings with the king or queen. The prime minister also participates in the House of Commons and represents the United Kingdom overseas. In September 2022, Boris Johnson stepped down as prime minister. Liz Truss took his place.

The prime minister receives guidance from ministers from the majority party, usually chosen from the House of Commons. The ministers carry out the country's laws and run the government. The most senior ministers form the cabinet, which decides policy on significant issues. The cabinet ministers also serve as the heads of several government departments.

JUDICIAL BRANCH

The judicial branch of the UK government enforces the country's laws. The UK court system is made up of a variety of courts, magistrates, and tribunals. Each type of court hears different cases based on the type and level of the case.

The Supreme Court of the United Kingdom, the highest court in the country, was created in 2009. Prior to that, the judicial branch was part of the legislature. In 2005, Parliament passed an act that would make the Supreme Court separate. Four years later, the UK Supreme Court began proceedings. The court hears appeals on the country's most important and high-profile civil and criminal cases.

UK Supreme Court justices wear ceremonial robes of black and gold for special occasions, such as the start of the legal year.

POLITICAL PARTIES

UK citizens vote in elections for MPs. The political party that wins the most seats in Parliament forms the government and is known as the majority party. By 2022, several political parties held seats in the UK Parliament. The main parties were the Conservative Party, Labour Party, and Liberal Democrats.

The Conservative Party generally holds center-right political views in UK politics. Among the party's major positions are the beliefs that businesses should not be regulated and free markets and individual achievements are the most effective drivers of economic growth. The Conservative Party often lobbies for tax cuts, as it believes lower taxes will help the UK economy grow. The party also supports a strong national defense and fiscal conservatism. The Conservative Party uses a drawing of an oak tree in red, white, and blue colors as its symbol. The oak tree is the national tree of England and represents strength and endurance.

The Labour Party generally holds more liberal, center-left views on policies. The party favors policies to redistribute wealth to help those who cannot support themselves, and it backs publicly funded education and health care. The Labour Party also supports more state control of essential industries. The Labour Party uses a red rose, the national flower of England, as its symbol.

The United Kingdom has many political parties. For instance, in the 2019 elections, members of 11 different political parties won seats in the House of Commons.[3]

The Liberal Democrats formed in 1988 from the merger of two smaller political parties. This party

Voting age varies between different UK countries. People have to be 18 to vote in parliamentary elections, but in Scotland people can vote at age 16 in local elections.

generally falls more in the center politically, between the more liberal Labour Party and the Conservative Party. The Liberal Democrats adopted the yellow bird of liberty symbol in 1989.

GOVERNMENTS IN SCOTLAND, WALES, AND NORTHERN IRELAND

All UK countries must follow the laws set by the UK Parliament, which is based in England. However, Scotland, Wales, and Northern Ireland also have governments that focus specifically on

The Welsh Parliament meets in the city of Cardiff.

their own countries. The UK Parliament has transferred various powers to these countries' national parliaments or assemblies.

The Scottish Parliament, the Welsh Parliament, and the Northern Ireland Assembly are responsible for specific duties in their respective countries. Instead of MPs in London, local politicians make important decisions on how Scotland, Wales, and Northern Ireland are governed. For instance, the politicians in these areas may be responsible for education, housing, and social

NATO

NATO is a multinational military alliance founded in 1949. The organization includes 30 member countries, including the United Kingdom and the United States. In the past, NATO conducted operations in Afghanistan, Iraq, Kosovo, and Somalia. In 2022, it also worked to deter aggression from Russia in Eastern Europe. NATO is a powerful organization because it promises to defend each participating country from military aggression. Article five of the NATO treaty says, "An armed attack against one or more [member states] in Europe or North America shall be considered an attack against them all."[5]

services. At the same time, the UK government is still responsible for establishing the United Kingdom's national policies on matters that have not been transferred to local authorities, such as foreign affairs, defense, social security, and larger economic and trade issues.

THE UK MILITARY

The military of the United Kingdom is one of the premier military forces worldwide. It includes the Royal Navy, the British Army, and the Royal Air Force. There are nearly 400,000 active and reserve members of the UK military.[4]

The British monarch is the commander in chief of the UK military in name. However, the British prime minister is actually in control of the UK military. The Ministry of Defense, created in 1964, oversees the United Kingdom's armed forces. The main focus of the United Kingdom's military is on ensuring national security from either foreign or domestic threats and participating in operations with partners in the North Atlantic Treaty Organization (NATO) and other allied militaries.

CHAPTER **SEVEN**

ECONOMICS

In the 1700s, the United Kingdom was the birthplace of the Industrial Revolution. It became one of the first countries to move from an agricultural economy to one that boomed with factories and mass production. Centuries later, the United Kingdom remains a highly industrialized nation.

In 2020, the United Kingdom produced $2.76 trillion in gross domestic product (GDP).[1] GDP is the amount of all income generated in a country from the sale of goods and services. It measures the economic strength of a country. When measured by GDP, the United Kingdom is the fifth-largest national economy in the world.[2]

The Industrial Revolution began in the United Kingdom and quickly spread to other countries.

CURRENCY

The national currency of the United Kingdom and its territories is the pound sterling, also called the pound. One pound can be divided into 100 pence. Pounds and pence are issued in several banknotes and coins. All UK coins and banknotes have the image of Queen Elizabeth II on one side. The pound is the world's oldest currency still in use. It was used as early as 775 CE in England, when it represented the equivalent of one pound (0.45 kg) in weight of silver.

The Bank of England issues the pound, which has an important role in London's foreign exchange trading hub. In 2022, the British pound was the fourth-most-traded currency globally. It is also a major global reserve currency. A global reserve currency is held in large amounts by central banks or other monetary authorities of foreign countries as part of their reserves. It can be used in international transactions and investments and is often considered a safe and stable currency.

While the pound is the official currency of the United Kingdom, some banks in Scotland and Northern Ireland issue their own pound banknotes.

INDUSTRIAL REVOLUTION

The Industrial Revolution was a period when a lot of work based on farming and handmade goods shifted to machine manufacturing and factories. The Industrial Revolution began in Great Britain in the mid-1700s. It eventually spread from Great Britain to Europe, the United States, and other parts of the world. The Industrial Revolution saw the invention of machines that did the work of hand tools, the use of steam power, and the rise of new energy sources such as electricity, petroleum, and the internal-combustion engine. The factory system, which relied on the division of labor to increase efficiency, also became popular.

The pound sterling is sometimes referred to as a quid.

They have the same value as the English pound. However, some notes can be used only in certain countries. For instance, Northern Ireland's notes can be used only in Northern Ireland.

MAJOR INDUSTRIES

The service industry in the United Kingdom is the largest contributor to its GDP. In 2020, services contributed 72.8 percent of GDP.[3] The UK service industry includes finance and business services, professional and scientific services, retail, food and beverage, and entertainment. It also includes service activities in hotels, restaurants, transportation, storage, real estate, education, arts, recreation, and more.

London is a busy city with around one million businesses.

Tourism is an important part of the UK economy and services sector. The United Kingdom has many historical and cultural attractions that bring people from around the world to visit. Tourists enjoy the country's rich architecture, archaeology, arts, culture, scenic landscapes, and historic sites. Millions of tourists visit London every year, seeing sights such as the Tower of London, the British Museum, the National Gallery, Westminster Abbey, Buckingham Palace, and Saint Paul's Cathedral. Vacationers travel to coastal spots and enjoy exploring the country's extensive coastline and national parks. In 2019, nearly 40.9 million international tourists visited the United Kingdom.[4]

AGRICULTURE IN THE UNITED KINGDOM

Agriculture is a small part of the UK economy, making up only 0.58 percent of the UK's GDP in 2020.[9] Major crops include potatoes and vegetables. The best farming land is typically located in lowland areas, with eastern regions most suitable for growing crops and western regions more commonly used for grazing livestock. Livestock is the most significant part of the United Kingdom's farming industry. The top agricultural products in the United Kingdom include milk, cattle meat, chicken meat, pig meat, wheat, sheep meat, potatoes, rapeseed, eggs, and sugar beets.

Those numbers significantly dropped in 2020 because of the worldwide coronavirus pandemic but were expected to rebound in 2022.

Outside of services, manufacturing industries contributed about 17 percent to the United Kingdom's GDP in 2020.[5] Some of the largest manufacturing sectors included food and beverage, chemicals and pharmaceuticals, textiles, clothing, glass, paper, automobiles, aircraft and aircraft parts, computers, and microelectronics. According to the World Economic Forum, the United Kingdom was the ninth-largest manufacturing country in 2018.[6] About one-fifth of England's workers have jobs in manufacturing.[7]

EXPORTS AND IMPORTS

In 2020, the United Kingdom was the world's eleventh-largest exporting country.[8] Its top exports included cars, packaged medications, and gas turbines. It was also the world's largest exporter of hard liquor, silver, brochures, and lard in 2020. The United Kingdom primarily exports its

Farmable land in the United Kingdom was estimated at 25.1 percent of the nation's overall land area in 2018.[11]

goods to the United States, Germany, Ireland, the Netherlands, and France.

The United Kingdom also imports many goods. These include preserved meat, fermented milk products, gold, cars, broadcasting equipment, and packaged medications. It imports mainly from Germany, China, the United States, the Netherlands, and France. Overall, the United Kingdom imports more goods and services than it exports. In 2020, the country exported $371 billion in goods, while it imported $610 billion in foreign goods.[10]

NATURAL RESOURCES

The United Kingdom's islands have several natural resources, including good land for crops and livestock, fossil fuels for energy, and minerals. The United Kingdom has large fossil fuel reserves of oil and natural gas. Oil reserves are primarily in the North Sea east of the Shetland Islands. Natural gas reserves are mainly located in the North Sea farther to the south.

Coal reserves are also scattered throughout Great Britain. However, much of the coal is in deep underground mines, making it expensive to extract. In 2020, natural gas and oil provided most of the United Kingdom's energy needs, supplemented by coal and nuclear power.

In addition, sand, gravel, and crushed rock are plentiful throughout the British Isles and are frequently used as raw materials by the construction industry. Clay and salt can be found in

Beef is one of the United Kingdom's main agricultural products.

northwestern England, while kaolin, also known as China clay, is located in Cornwall. The United Kingdom also has deposits of minerals such as copper and iron ore. However, many minerals are no longer mined in the United Kingdom because importing them from other countries is cheaper.

The Tower Bridge in London can be adjusted to let large ships sail past.

TRANSPORTATION

People and goods move throughout the United Kingdom by roads, railways, ports, and airports. Numerous ports around the British Isles handle goods and passengers traveling to and from

THE CHANNEL TUNNEL

The Channel Tunnel was completed in 1994 and was seen as an amazing engineering accomplishment. The tunnel runs underneath the English Channel and connects Great Britain and France. Digging of the tunnel began in the late 1980s, and workers used enormous tunnel-boring machines that cut through the chalk rock, collected the debris, and removed it. As the machines dug, the sides of the tunnel were lined with concrete to help the tunnel withstand enormous pressure from above and to waterproof it. In 1991, the two sides met in the middle. Three years later, the Channel Tunnel officially opened.

the country. Some major UK ports include Liverpool, Southampton, Clydeport, Manchester, and Bristol.

London's main airports, Heathrow and Gatwick, are two of the busiest in the world. Heathrow alone served 80.1 million passengers in 2018 and carried 1.87 million tons (1.7 million metric tons) of cargo.[12] Other busy UK airports include Glasgow in Scotland, Ringway in Manchester, and Aldergrove in Belfast.

The United Kingdom has thousands of miles of rail track. One of the most remarkable is a high-speed rail tunnel that travels under the English Channel for 31 miles (50 km).[13] Known as the Channel Tunnel, or Chunnel, it connects Folkestone, England, with Sangatte, France.

Cars, buses, trucks, and motorcycles travel on the miles of highways and paved roads that crisscross the United Kingdom. In larger cities such as London, the traffic on the streets can cause congestion and slowdowns. Within London, many travelers prefer to use the London Underground train system to avoid traffic on the city's streets.

CHAPTER **EIGHT**

THE UNITED KINGDOM TODAY

Each UK country has its own culture and identity that many of the local people cherish. Even within each country, different regions and cities have their own ways of doing things. For example, many people say that individuals from Northern England are more direct and outspoken than those from Southern England.

Regardless of its regional differences, the United Kingdom is a multicultural country. Its people are generally respectful of different beliefs, religions, and cultures. Many people from other countries travel and

Migrants to the United Kingdom contribute to the nation's rich cultural diversity.

make their homes in the United Kingdom because they find it a welcoming place to live and work.

DAILY LIFE IN THE UNITED KINGDOM

Daily life for many teens in the United Kingdom includes going to school, hanging out with friends, listening to music, going to movies, playing video games, and shopping for the latest fashions in stores and online. They text, make videos, and post on social media with smartphones.

The average UK family lives in a house or an apartment, called a flat. Most houses in the United Kingdom are built with stones or bricks from local areas. Some houses are semidetached, meaning two houses share a single wall. In more rural areas, homes are fully detached and often have front and back yards, called gardens. Also, in more rural areas, some people live in traditional cottages or bungalows.

Terraced houses are some of the most iconic types of homes in the United Kingdom and are similar to rowhomes or townhouses in the United States. Terraced houses are connected by a

AFTERNOON TEA

In Great Britain, afternoon tea is a time-honored tradition. The custom began in the 1800s with the seventh Duchess of Bedford. In her time, lunch was served early, while supper was ready very late. Hungry between the two meals, the duchess began to take tea and a light meal in the afternoon between three and four o'clock. Soon, she began to invite her friends to join her. The duchess's tea habit quickly became a beloved tradition throughout the country.

wall on each side, which creates an unbroken row of houses along a street. This type of housing structure saves a lot of space and is popular in urban areas.

Flats are a common type of home in the United Kingdom, particularly in cities. These homes are built with the goal of saving space while also offering people a convenient place to live. Flats can be either rented from a landlord or owned. Flats are often more affordable than detached or terraced houses and are ideal living spaces for single people, couples, or small families.

One of the biggest differences between UK and American and European housing is size. Average homes in the United Kingdom are typically smaller than average homes in both Europe and the United States. According to the UK Office for National Statistics, the average home in the United Kingdom is one-third the size of the average US home.[1]

In 2020, the life expectancy in the United Kingdom was almost 83 years for women and 79 years for men.[2]

EDUCATION

The UK education system is divided into four main stages: primary education, secondary education, further education, and higher education. The law requires children ages five to 16 to attend school. Primary education begins at age five and continues until about age 11. Then students move on to secondary education between the ages of 11 and 16. At age 16, students sit for the General Certificate of Secondary Education (GCSE) test. This exam tests students in different subjects.

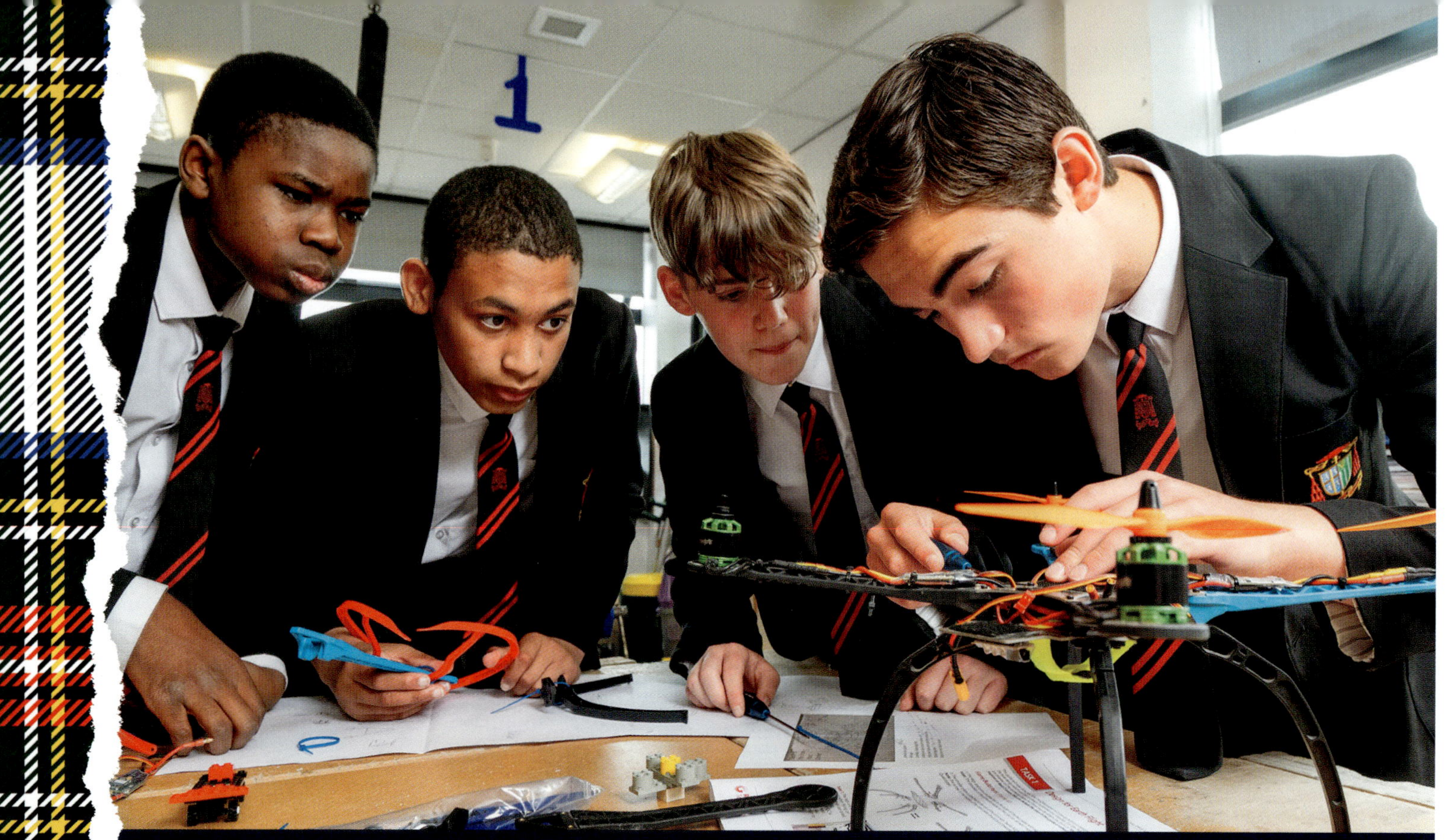

Students in the United Kingdom get educational opportunities that allow them to succeed in adulthood.

For each subject passed, the student earns a GCSE. In Scotland, students participate in a separate exam system.

Once students have taken their GCSEs, they can choose to continue their education or finish school and enter the workforce. Students who choose to further their education may enter vocational programs or start a two-year program that leads to A (Advanced) level examinations. Students studying for A levels specialize in three to four subjects, which often are related to what they want to study at a university.

Some students choose to attend a university for higher education. A university often looks at its applicants' GCSEs to determine if they will fit in well at the school. Several UK universities are well-known and respected around the world. The University of Oxford and the University of Cambridge have educated students since the 1100s and 1200s, respectively. In Scotland, the universities of St. Andrews, Glasgow, Aberdeen, and Edinburgh have instructed students since the 1400s and 1500s. In addition to universities, the United Kingdom offers hundreds of other higher education institutions, including technical, art, and commercial colleges.

LONDON'S THEATERS

London's theater district in the city's West End rivals Broadway in New York City for quality shows. On any given day, visitors can choose from hundreds of shows to see. And there's entertainment for everyone, including Shakespeare plays, musicals, comedies, thrillers, cutting-edge modern shows, revivals featuring movie stars, and more. Many productions draw big-name celebrities who want to challenge their acting skills.

HOBBIES AND RECREATION

People in the United Kingdom often enjoy traditional hobbies, with drawing, reading, walking, eating out, and gardening being some of the most popular. In 2020, a poll of 2,000 adults in the country found that they enjoyed an average of three hobbies per week and spent more than eight

The Old Course at St. Andrews Links in Scotland is the oldest golf course in the world. It was established in 1552.

hours a week on them.[3] The survey also found that hobbies such as cooking, baking, and watching movies were popular.

European soccer has a passionate following. About 11 million people play the game themselves. When it comes to soccer fans, 19 million people cheer on professional teams in televised matches.[4]

With so many excellent courses across the country, golf is another popular pastime in the United Kingdom. England has the highest number of registered golf courses in Europe, with 1,888 in 2018.[5] The second-place country, Germany, had less than half that number. Scotland, Ireland, and Wales also boast hundreds of beautiful golf courses. It is not surprising that many people in the United Kingdom play golf.

A number of people in the United Kingdom are outdoor enthusiasts. They enjoy various outdoor leisure activities such as hiking, bicycling, exploring national parks, camping, surfing, canoeing, kayaking, and more. In Snowdonia National Park in Wales, climbers worldwide come to challenge themselves on the mountains.

HOGMANAY

In Scotland, Hogmanay is a New Year's celebration lasting from December 31 to January 2. It is thought to be good luck if the first person to enter a Scottish home on New Year's Day is a man, and it is believed to be bad luck if a woman is the first to enter the house. This superstition led to a tradition called first footing, in which a male friend enters a home first on New Year's Day and gives the homeowner a small ceremonial gift. To ensure the best luck, the man ideally would have dark hair.

CELEBRATIONS AND FESTIVALS

Many celebrations occur in the United Kingdom every year. These include royal traditions, religious celebrations, and modern festivals. These special occasions have developed over the country's long and rich history and are enjoyed by many residents today.

The Notting Hill Carnival is one of the biggest street festivals in Europe and takes place in London at the end of August. The carnival was first organized in 1964 by Rhaune Laslett, a woman who wanted to bring together people of different races and classes in London. It has since evolved into a massive celebration of Caribbean culture in the United Kingdom and features dancing, live music, and fantastic food.

In the Christian faith, Ash Wednesday marks the beginning of Lent, a 40-day period of fasting before Easter. In the United Kingdom, many people celebrate the day before, called Shrove Tuesday, by eating pancakes as a last indulgence before Lent. Some communities even hold pancake races where people race while flipping pancakes in a frying pan. The winner crosses the finish line first without dropping or burning the pancake.

Trooping the Colour is an annual ceremony that marks the sovereign's official birthday and has been held annually for more than 260 years. For instance, celebrations for Queen Elizabeth II used to be held in June to honor her birthday. Each year, more than 1,400 soldiers, 200 horses, and 400 musicians met in London to form a parade for this ceremony.[6]

In Wales, the Eisteddfod festival takes place in August each year. It celebrates the language and culture of that country. People set up stands with food and products to purchase. There are also music and arts and crafts for people to enjoy.

DEALING WITH CHALLENGES

Like every nation in the world, the United Kingdom faces modern-day challenges and keeps an eye out for future struggles. One challenge was the COVID-19 pandemic that emerged in late 2019. To slow the spread of the virus that causes the deadly COVID-19 disease, the United Kingdom and other countries worldwide instituted lockdowns for citizens and closed businesses, schools,

The royal family's Household Cavalry Mounted Regiment takes part in Trooping the Colour.

Like many people around the world, people in the United Kingdom wore masks in public to protect themselves from COVID-19.

and borders to varying degrees. The UK economy slowed and people reported more mental health problems.

Another challenge the country faces is the rise of hate crimes. These are crimes committed against people based on their race or ethnicity, religious beliefs, sexual orientation, whether they have a disability, and whether they are transgender. Between 2020 and 2021, England and Wales reported an increase in these types of crimes. Hate crimes can take many forms, such as assault, harassment, and damage to property. Some UK leaders are looking for ways to end hate crimes so people can live without fear.

There was also a spike in hate crimes and racist rhetoric following the Brexit vote in 2016. In addition to tackling hate at home, leaders must think about how the United Kingdom's departure from the European Union will affect the country. Business leaders fear that Brexit could harm London's ability to do business with Europe. Some people are concerned that it may become more difficult for them to travel, live, and work in Europe without EU membership. And economists worry that the United Kingdom will suffer if trade with European partners declines.

Despite the serious challenges it faces, the United Kingdom remains one of the world's most influential nations. Tourists continue to visit the country and take in its sights. With its natural beauty, heritage, culture, and traditions, the future looks bright for the United Kingdom and its people.

ESSENTIAL **FACTS**

OFFICIAL NAME: UNITED KINGDOM OF GREAT BRITAIN AND NORTHERN IRELAND

GEOGRAPHY

Area: 93,410 square miles (241,930 sq km)

Highest Elevation: Ben Nevis in Scotland at 4,413 feet (1,345 m)

Lowest Elevation: The Fens in eastern England at –13 feet (–4 m)

PEOPLE

Population: 67.7 million (2022 est.)

Most Populous City: London (9.426 million)

Ethnic Groups: White, Black, Indian, Pakistani

Religions: Christianity, Islam, Hinduism, Judaism

GOVERNMENT

Type of Government: Constitutional monarchy

Capital: London

Head of State: King or queen

Head of Government: Prime minister

Legislature: UK Parliament

ECONOMY

Currency: Pound sterling

Major Industries: Manufacturing, banking, insurance, business

Natural Resources: Coal, petroleum, natural gas, iron ore, lead, zinc, gold, tin, limestone, salt, clay, chalk, gypsum, potash, silica sand, slate, farmland

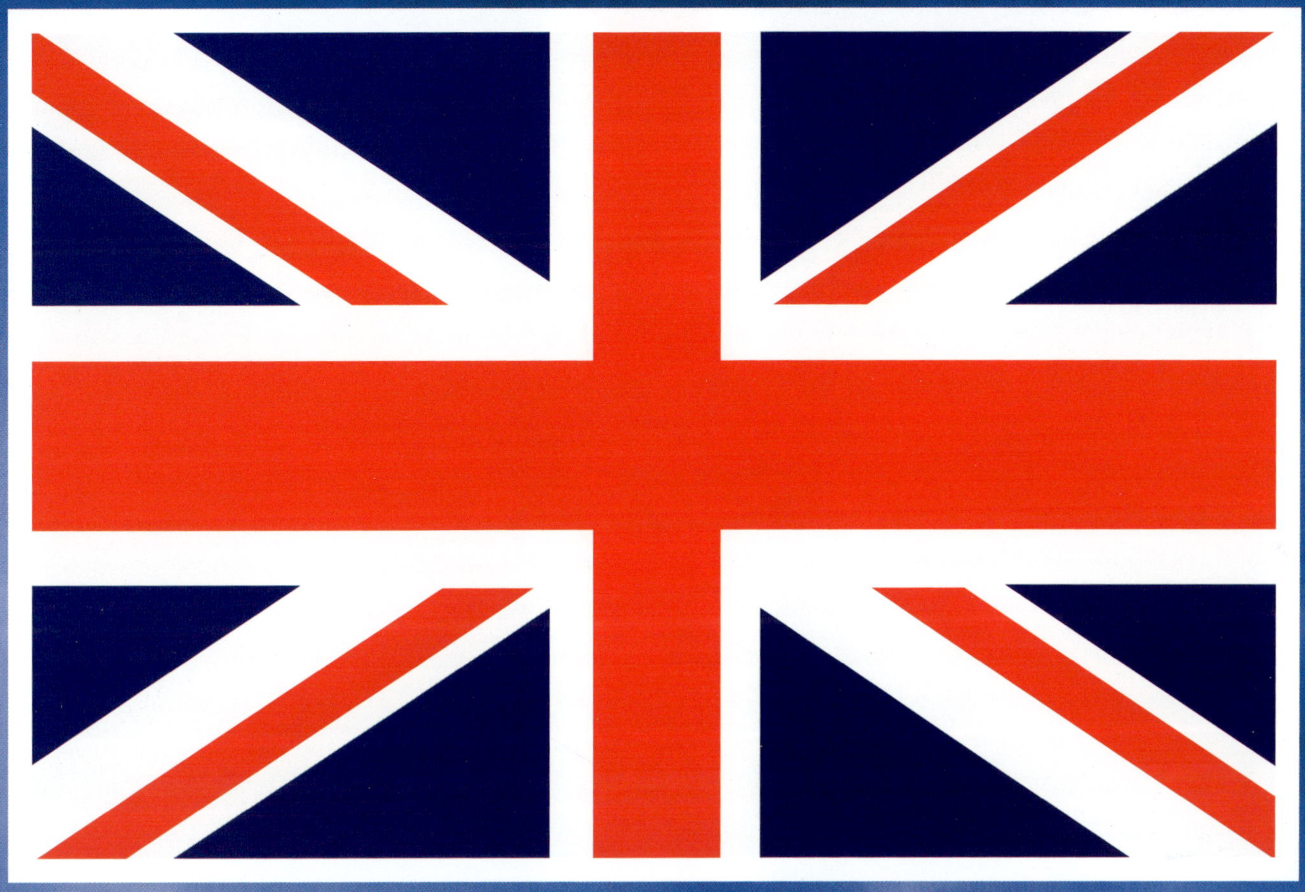

NATIONAL SYMBOLS

National Anthem: "God Save the King"

National Birds: Robin (England), oystercatcher (Northern Ireland), golden eagle (Scotland), and the red kite (Wales)

National Flowers: Rose (England), shamrock (Northern Ireland), thistle (Scotland), and daffodil (Wales)

GLOSSARY

ARCHAEOLOGIST
A person who studies human history by examining artifacts and other physical remains.

CLIMATE
The long-term weather pattern in an area.

CRICKET
A bat and ball game played on a field with two teams of 11 players each.

EXPORT
To sell goods to another country.

HABITAT
The natural environment of an organism.

IMPORT
To buy goods from another country.

INFRASTRUCTURE
The physical structures, such as roads, railways, and power plants, that make it possible for a city or nation to function.

ISLET
A very small island.

MIGRANT
A person who moves from one place to another, often to find work or better living conditions.

NATURAL RESOURCES
Resources supplied by nature that can be used in industry.

NOMADIC
Moving from one place to another.

PENINSULA
A piece of land projecting out into a body of water.

TEMPERATE
Having mild temperatures.

ADDITIONAL **RESOURCES**

SELECTED BIBLIOGRAPHY

Riches, Christopher. *A Guide to Countries of the World*. Oxford University Press, 2016.

Steves, Rick. *Rick Steves Great Britain*. Hachette Book Group, 2020.

"Story of England." *English Heritage*, n.d., english-heritage.org.uk. Accessed 4 Apr. 2022.

FURTHER READINGS

Ewart, Tim. *Queen Elizabeth II: A Celebration of Her Life and Reign*. Welbeck, 2018.

Karpovich, Todd. *Manchester United*. Abdo, 2018.

McKinney, Donna B. *Brexit*. Abdo, 2021.

ONLINE RESOURCES

To learn more about the United Kingdom, please visit **abdobooklinks.com** or scan this QR code. These links are routinely monitored and updated to provide the most current information available.

MORE INFORMATION

For more information on this subject, contact or visit the following organizations:

English Heritage
The Engine House
Fire Fly Ave.
Swindon SN2 2EH
english-heritage.org.uk
English Heritage is a charity organization that manages more than 400 historic monuments, buildings, and other places. These include prehistoric sites, medieval castles, Roman forts, and country houses in the United Kingdom.

National Museum Cardiff
Cathays Park
Cardiff, Wales
CF10 3NP
museum.wales/cardiff
The National Museum Cardiff features world-class art and engaging events and exhibits. Visitors can learn about the history of Wales while touring the museum.

SOURCE **NOTES**

CHAPTER 1. A TOUR OF THE UNITED KINGDOM

1. "London Underground." *Encyclopedia Britannica*, 19 Jan. 2011, britannica.com. Accessed 3 June 2022.
2. "London Underground."
3. "Building Stonehenge." *English Heritage*, n.d., english-heritage.org.uk. Accessed 3 June 2022.
4. Wynne Parry. "In Photos: A Walk through Stonehenge." *Livescience*, 2 May 2012, livescience.com. Accessed 3 June 2022.
5. "Researchers: Stonehenge Started as Huge Graveyard." *USA Today*, 9 Mar. 2013, usatoday.com. Accessed 3 June 2022.
6. "United Kingdom." *CIA World Factbook*, 31 May 2022, cia.gov. Accessed 3 June 2022.
7. "British Empire Overview." *National Archives*, n.d., nationalarchives.gov.uk. Accessed 3 June 2022.

CHAPTER 2. GEOGRAPHY

1. "United Kingdom." *CIA World Factbook*, 31 May 2022, cia.gov. Accessed 3 June 2022.
2. Ulric M. Spencer. "United Kingdom." *Encyclopedia Britannica*, 1 June 2022, britannica.com. Accessed 3 June 2022.
3. Peter Kellner. "England." *Encyclopedia Britannica*, 15 Dec. 2021, britannica.com. Accessed 3 June 2022.
4. "Ben Nevis." *Ben Nevis*, n.d., bennevis.co.uk. Accessed 3 June 2022.
5. "Snowdon." *Encyclopedia Britannica*, 6 Jan. 2015, britannica.com. Accessed 3 June 2022.
6. "Slieve Donard." *Encyclopedia Britannica*, 18 Nov. 2014, britannica.com. Accessed 3 June 2022.
7. "Lough Neagh." *Encyclopedia Britannica*, 23 Aug. 2013, britannica.com. Accessed 3 June 2022.
8. John Misachi. "Longest Rivers in the United Kingdom." *World Atlas*, 25 Apr. 2017, worldatlas.com. Accessed 3 June 2022.
9. "United Kingdom," *CIA World Factbook.*
10. "Monthly Average Daily Temperatures in the United Kingdom (UK) from 2015 to 2021." *Statista*, 14 Feb. 2022, statista.com. Accessed 3 June 2022.

CHAPTER 3. PLANTS AND ANIMALS

1. "UK Species." *Natural History Museum*, n.d., nhm.ac.uk. Accessed 3 June 2022.
2. Brendan Montague. "How Rewilding Britain Could Absorb Even More CO2 Than Tree Planting." *World Economic Forum*, 17 Sept. 2020, weforum.org. Accessed 3 June 2022.
3. Michael Charles Prestwich. "United Kingdom." *Encyclopedia Britannica*, 1 June 2022, britannica.com. Accessed 3 June 2022.
4. "Who We Are." *Moorland Association*, n.d., moorlandassociation.org. Accessed 3 June 2022.
5. "Heathland." *Young People's Trust for the Environment*, n.d., ypte.org.uk. Accessed 3 June 2022.
6. Josh Davis. "UK Has 'Led the World' in Destroying the Natural Environment." *Natural History Museum*, 26 Sept. 2020, nhm.ac.uk. Accessed 3 June 2022.
7. Damian Carrington. "Quarter of Native UK Mammals at Imminent Risk of Extinction." *Guardian*, 30 July 2020, theguardian.com. Accessed 3 June 2022.
8. "10 Things about the UK's Urban Wildlife." *Oxford Student*, 31 Oct. 2019, oxfordstudent.com. Accessed 3 June 2022.
9. Damian Carrington. "Populations of UK's Most Important Wildlife Have Plummeted Since 1970." *Guardian*, 3 Oct. 2019, theguardian.com. Accessed 3 June 2022.
10. Josh Davis. "The State of Nature: 41 Percent of UK Species Have Declined Since 1970s." *Natural History Museum*, 4 Oct. 2019, nhm.ac.uk. Accessed 3 June 2022.

CHAPTER 4. HISTORY

1. Jeff Wallenfeldt. "The Troubles." *Encyclopedia Britannica*, 21 Aug. 2020, britannica.com. Accessed 3 June 2022.
2. "The Fallen." *UK Parliament*, n.d., parliament.uk. Accessed 3 June 2022.

CHAPTER 5. PEOPLE AND CULTURE

1. "Diversity in the UK." *DiversityUK*, n.d., diversityuk.org. Accessed 3 June 2022.
2. "Language." *Study UK*, n.d., study-uk.britishcouncil.org. Accessed 3 June 2022.
3. Harriet Sherwood. "UK Secularism on Rise as More Than Half Say They Have No Religion." *Guardian*, 10 July 2019, theguardian.com. Accessed 3 June 2022.
4. "William Shakespeare Biography." *Shakespeare Birthplace Trust*, n.d., shakespeare.org.uk. Accessed 3 June 2022.

CHAPTER 6. POLITICS

1. "Diverse Experience." *UK Parliament*, n.d., parliament.uk. Accessed 3 June 2022.
2. "House of Commons." *UK Parliament*, n.d., parliament.uk. Accessed 3 June 2022.
3. "Political Parties in Parliament." *UK Parliament*, n.d., parliament.uk. Accessed 3 June 2022.
4. "Introduction to the Armed Forces of the United Kingdom." *British Military Essentials*, n.d., navycs.com. Accessed 3 June 2022.
5. Jonathan Masters. "What Is NATO?" *Council on Foreign Relations*, 4 May 2022, cfr.org. Accessed 3 June 2022.

SOURCE **NOTES** CONTINUED

CHAPTER 7. ECONOMICS

1. Caleb Silver. "The Top 25 Economies in the World." *Investopedia*, 22 Dec. 2021, investopedia.com. Accessed 3 June 2022.
2. "The World's Largest Economies." *World Data*, n.d., worlddata.info. Accessed 3 June 2022.
3. Aaron O'Neill. "United Kingdom: Distribution of Gross Domestic Product (GDP) across Economic Sectors from 2010 to 2020." *Statista*, 15 Feb. 2022, statista.com. Accessed 3 June 2022.
4. "Number of Overseas Resident Visits to the United Kingdom (UK) from 2002 to 2020, with a Forecast Until 2022." *Statista*, 23 Feb. 2022, statista.com. Accessed 3 June 2022.
5. O'Neill, "United Kingdom."
6. Felix Richter. "These Are the Top 10 Manufacturing Countries in the World." *World Economic Forum*, 25 Feb. 2020, weforum.org. Accessed 3 June 2022.
7. Peter Kellner. "England." *Encyclopedia Britannica*, 15 Dec. 2021, britannica.com. Accessed 3 June 2022.
8. "United Kingdom." *OEC*, n.d., oec.world. Accessed 3 June 2022.
9. O'Neill, "United Kingdom."
10. "United Kingdom," *OEC*.
11. "United Kingdom." *CIA World Factbook*, 31 May 2022, cia.gov. Accessed 3 June 2022.
12. "Facts and Figures." *Heathrow*, n.d., heathrow.com. Accessed 3 June 2022.
13. Timothy L. Gall and Derek M. Gleason, eds. "United Kingdom." *World History*, n.d., link.gale.com. Accessed 3 June 2022.

CHAPTER 8. THE UNITED KINGDOM TODAY

1. Thomas Colson. "English Homes Are Nearly a Third of the Size of American Homes." *Business Insider*, 14 Oct. 2017, businessinsider.com. Accessed 3 June 2022.

2. "National Life Tables—Life Expectancy in the UK: 2018 to 2020." *Office for National Statistics*, 23 Sept. 2021, ons.gov.uk. Accessed 3 June 2022.

3. Astrid Hall. "UK Is Still a Nation of Traditionalists When It Comes to Pastimes, Poll Finds." *Independent*, 16 Oct. 2020, independent.co.uk. Accessed 3 June 2022.

4. Deborah Preston. "Most Popular Leisure Activities in the UK." *Travel with a Mate*, n.d., travelwithamate.com. Accessed 3 June 2022.

5. David Lange. "Number of Registered Golf Courses in England from 2014 to 2018." *Statista*, 19 Nov. 2020. statista.com. Accessed 3 June 2022.

6. "What Is Trooping the Colour?" *Royal*, n.d., royal.uk. Accessed 3 June 2022.

INDEX

ABOUT THE **AUTHOR**

CARLA MOONEY

Carla Mooney is a graduate of the University of Pennsylvania with a degree in economics. Today, she writes for young people and is the author of many books for young adults and children. Mooney enjoys traveling to new places around the world.